C000178332

dog treats

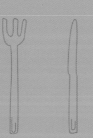

dog treats
fun • facts • food

Caroline Davis and Emma Hawkins

hamlyn

First published in Great Britain in 2002 by Hamlyn, a division of
Octopus Publishing Group Ltd, 2–4 Heron Quays, London E14 4JP

ISBN 0 600 60718 6

A CIP catalogue record for this book is available from the British Library

Printed and bound in China

10 9 8 7 6 5 4 3 2 1

Notes for American readers

Both metric and imperial measurements have been used in
all recipes. Use one set of measurements only, and not a
mixture of both.

Standard level spoon measurements are used in all recipes.
1 tablespoon = one 15 ml spoon
1 teaspoon = one 5 ml spoon

Ovens should be pre-heated to the specified temperature –
if using a fan-assisted oven, follow the manufacturer's
instructions for adjusting the time and temperature.

UK	US
vegetable spread	margarine
plain flour	all-purpose flour
minced beef	ground beef
sultanas	golden raisins
demerara sugar	raw sugar crystals

what's inside

- ## tasty tidbits
  30 simple savoury and sweet recipes for everyday doggy training treats and meals for special occasions

  Plus...

- ### prized possessions Famous
  people with a passion for dogs

- ### understanding your dog
  How to read canine body language and communicate with your pet

- ### historical dogs Four-legged
  legends in fact and fiction

- ### canine quotations Who
  said what about man's best friend

- ### pooches in print Poems,
  prose and literary connections

- ### dog stars Past and
  present idols from the world of entertainment

- ### origins of dog sayings
  Discover the sources of well-known canine clichés and proverbs

- ### perfect presents Easy-to-
  make gifts for a pampered pooch

- ### doggy trivia Fascinating
  facts about dogs past, present and fictional

- ### play time Fun activities for
  dogs and owners

- ### top tips Helpful hints on
  canine care and training

introduction

If you love dogs, you are sure to treasure this compilation of all things canine. From fascinating doggy facts and wholesome recipes to canine quotations and homemade presents, this book is filled with more top tips than your pet's had bones, and celebrates the absolute joy that a dog can bring to your life.

watching waistlines

There's nothing more likely to make your dog's tail wag than a tasty food treat. But you must be careful not to offer your dog too many gourmet goodies (even though those pleading eyes can be hard to resist). Obesity can become a problem, especially for dogs that love their food but are not keen on burning off excess calories with exercise.

Yesterday I was a dog. Today I'm a dog. Tomorrow I'll probably still be a dog. – Sigh! – There's so little hope for advancement.

Snoopy, cartoon dog

made with love

Dog Treats provides plenty of special recipes you can make quickly and easily at home. And you will have the added benefit of knowing that your homemade dog snacks are packed with natural goodness and don't contain artificial colourings and preservatives. So, why not treat your furry friend to a delicious and wholesome delicacy that you have lovingly prepared?

pooches in print

The dog

The truth I do not stretch or shove
When I state the dog is full of love.
I've also proved by actual test
A wet dog is the lovingest.

Ogden Nash, writer of humorous verse (1902–71)

puppy pick-me-up

A munchy, crunchy, healthy and wholesome dish that you can serve at any time of the day for the dog in your life.

1 wheat breakfast biscuit, crumbled
handful of bran strands
handful of bran flakes, crumbled
4 tablespoons low-fat natural yogurt
1 tablespoon liquid honey
thin slices of fruit such as apple, banana,
    grapes, strawberries or mango, to decorate

1 Mix all the ingredients together and transfer to a serving dish.
2 Decorate the mixture with slices of fruit.
3 Serve for breakfast, brunch, lunch or any other time you want to treat your pet.

What counts is not necessarily the size of the dog in the fight – it's the size of the fight in the dog.

Dwight D. Eisenhower, US president (1890–1969)

top tips

Many dogs crave fruits and vegetables for the natural sugars, vitamins and minerals they provide. Hypersensitive dogs in particular may benefit from a fresh food diet that includes an abundance of fruits and vegetables. The juicy crunchiness of fruit and vegetables is great for their teeth, too.

To make a delicious doggy salad, you will need 2 baby carrots, 1 small stick of broccoli, 2 cauliflower florets, a handful of young peas in a pod, 2 Brussels sprouts, 2 cherry tomatoes, a handful of dessert apple chunks and 6 green or red seedless grapes. Wash all the ingredients and mix them together in a serving bowl. Top the salad with fresh parsley and mint sprigs for fresh breath.

'It's a dog's life'

Meaning: A miserable and bleak existence.
This saying is thought to date back to the 16th century when life was tough for our canine chums. It is attributed to Dutch Renaissance humanist Desiderius Erasmus (1466–1536), who wrote: 'The most part of folkes calleth it a miserable life, or a dogges life...'

10

dog stars

Scooby Doo, the cartoon Great Dane, first hit US television screens in 1969. The canine detective's name was supposedly inspired by Frank Sinatra when he sang the phrase 'scooby dooby do' in the song 'Strangers in the Night'.

no-fleas-on-me fancies

If Fido's got friends you'd
rather not meet, then a couple
of these crunchy, mouth-watering
morsels a day will help keep
them away.

¼ beef stock cube
1 tablespoon boiling water
1 tablespoon vegetable oil
½ small egg, beaten
25 g/1 oz/¼ cup plain flour
25 g/1 oz/¼ cup plain wholemeal flour
25 g/1 oz/⅓ cup porridge (rolled) oats
25 g/1 oz/⅛ cup cornmeal
6 crushed brewer's yeast tablets or
    1 teaspoon brewer's yeast powder
1 tablespoon garlic powder
extra flour, for rolling out

1 Pre-heat the oven to 200°C/400°F/Gas Mark 6. Grease a baking
   tray or use a nonstick one.
2 Dissolve the stock cube in the boiling water and allow to cool.
   Mix the oil, egg and stock together.
3 Put all the dry ingredients into a bowl and mix together. Gradually
   add the stock mixture and work into a dough.
4 Roll out the dough on a floured surface to about 5 mm/¼ inch
   thick. Use cookie cutters to cut out shapes and place them on
   the baking tray.
5 Bake for 40 minutes or until golden brown. Cool on a rack.

hal's heroes

These meaty little nibbles are
the perfect training treats -
your dog'll do anything for one.

375 g/12 oz ox or lambs' liver
1.5 litres/2½ pints/7 cups cold water

1 Pre-heat the oven to 140°C/275°F/Gas
   Mark 1. Grease a baking tray or use a
   nonstick one.
2 Put the liver in a pan with the water, bring
   to the boil and simmer until cooked
   through (approximately 30 minutes).
3 Drain the water into a plastic jug and save
   it in the refrigerator to add to regular
   mixer feeds.
4 Allow the liver to cool, then cut into
   1 cm/½ inch pieces. Place the pieces on
   the baking tray and cook in the bottom
   of the oven for 1 hour.
5 Allow to cool, then serve as required.
   Store in the refrigerator and use within
   three days.

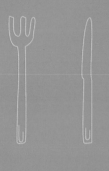

12

play time

Hide and seek: Get your dog to use his nose by playing a canine version of hide and seek. Put a tasty tidbit or his favourite toy in a place where he can easily find it, such as by a plant pot in the garden or a chair leg indoors. Do this while he is watching. Tell him to 'find' and, when he does, praise him. Gradually make it harder by hiding the items in more difficult places. Once he gets the hang of the game, put him in another room when you hide the goodies so that he has to use his tracking skills.

prized possessions

Sugar

Actress Elizabeth Taylor's companion is a Maltese called Sugar. The movie star is so devoted to her pet that she takes Sugar everywhere, including star-studded award shows. Elizabeth stayed away from the UK for seven years because of the country's quarantine laws, which would have seen the small dog parted from the actress for six months.

canine kebab

These devilishly delectable doggy dainties will ensure your pooch remains your number-one fan.

325 g/11 oz kidneys, quartered
6 cherry tomatoes, halved
8 button mushrooms

1 Pre-heat the grill until it is red hot.
2 Place the kidneys and vegetables on a long skewer (a skewer with a wooden handle will be easier to turn).
3 Grill the kebab, turning frequently, until it is cooked through (the juices should run clear).
4 Allow to cool and store in the refrigerator. Give pieces of the kebab to your dog as a treat when required.

top tips

Raw beef bones are the ultimate yummy tidbits. They are rich in minerals and can help to clean your dog's teeth. Choose bones that are thick and fresh, have shreds of cartilage and fibrous meaty tissue attached, and come from a safe source such as a reputable butcher. Be careful if you give your dog a knucklebone because it can disintegrate into small pieces and cause choking. Try to avoid dry-roasted bones because they are prone to splintering, which can lead to mouth and stomach injuries. Remember, the size of the bone should be appropriate to the size of the dog.

You want a friend in Washington? Get a dog.

**Harry S. Truman,
US president (1884–1972)**

Types of bark

- **Strong and steady barking:** Alert! This is a warning to let you know that a stranger is coming. It's not intended to scare the intruder away but to call for back-up.
- **Fast and furious barking:** What on earth is that? Your pet has spotted something he doesn't recognize – could be a running rabbit or a vacuum cleaner.
- **Single high-pitched bark:** I want it now! Normally accompanied by tail wagging, this is his way of telling you he wants something – could be dinner, a toy or a cuddle.
- **Whining/high-pitched and urgent:** A stress reliever. Dogs need to relieve tension just like humans and this is their noisy way of doing so. This often happens when a dog is left alone.

16

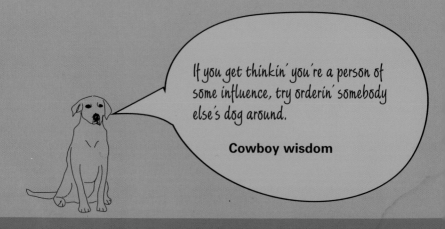

If you get thinkin' you're a person of some influence, try orderin' somebody else's dog around.

Cowboy wisdom

kennel kiss cakes

Banish foul dog breath for ever
with these mouth-freshening
cookies. They'll keep your dog's
kisses sweet, not sour.

125 g/4 oz/1 cup plain white flour
25 g/1 oz/⅛ cup cornmeal
2 tablespoons dried mint
3 tablespoons dried parsley
50 ml/2 fl oz/¼ cup water
6 tablespoons vegetable oil
extra flour, for rolling out
sunflower seeds

1 Pre-heat the oven to 180°C/350°F/Gas
  Mark 4. Grease a baking tray or use a
  nonstick one.
2 Combine the flour, cornmeal, mint and
  parsley in a large bowl. Add the water and
  oil and mix thoroughly.
3 Roll out to 5 mm/¼ inch thick on a floured
  surface and cut into shapes with cookie
  cutters.
4 Decorate the shapes with sunflower
  seeds and place them on the baking tray.
  Bake for 40 minutes until lightly browned.
5 Allow the biscuits to dry out in a warm
  place (on top of a radiator is ideal) for
  several hours. Store them in an airtight
  container to keep them crisp.

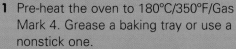

luxury liver cookies

It's not just humans who love cookies. These delicious liver-flavoured ones are perfect for a pup's garden party.

50 g/2 oz/½ cup plain wholemeal flour
25 g/1 oz/¼ cup plain white flour
75 g/3 oz/⅓ cup cornmeal
double handful of crushed cornflakes
double handful of sunflower seeds
2 tablespoons dried skimmed milk
1 heaped tablespoon low-fat sunflower spread
double handful of finely chopped Hal's Heroes
  (see page 12)
7 tablespoons cold water
1 egg, beaten
extra flour, for rolling out

1 Pre-heat the oven to 200°C/400°F/Gas Mark 6. Grease a baking tray or use a nonstick one.
2 Put all the ingredients (except the Hal's Heroes, water, egg and extra flour) in a bowl and rub together until the mixture resembles breadcrumbs.
3 Add the Hal's Heroes and water and stir to make a dough.
4 Press out the dough with floury palms on a floured surface until it is 5 mm/¼ inch thick. Use cookie cutters to cut out shapes.
5 Place the shapes on the baking tray, brush lightly with beaten egg and bake until golden brown. Allow to cool on a wire rack.

18

Canine crooner

The most unique characteristic of the New Guinea Singing Dog is its dramatic ability to vary the pitch of its howl. The animal does not bark repetitively but has a complex vocal behaviour, including yelps, whines and single-note howls.

top tips

Introduce a regular physical examination to your dog's routine. Check his eyes (should be bright and shiny), ears (no dark wax or parasites), teeth (free of tartar and gums should be pink), nose (moist and no discharge) and general well-being (no weight gain or loss and no lumps or bumps). Examine your dog a couple of times a month so that you can identify any developing health problems quickly. If you reward your dog when you've finished, he'll eagerly look forward to his next physical.

apple snacks

Fat- and salt-free, these munchy morsels are top dollar in the doggy snack stakes.

1 dessert apple

1 Pre-heat the oven to 140°C/275°F/Gas Mark 1. Line a baking tray with baking parchment.
2 Wash and core the apple, then slice very thinly. Place the slices, without overlapping them, on the baking tray.
3 Place the tray on the bottom shelf of the oven and bake for approximately 45 minutes or until the slices are light brown and crispy. Turn two or three times while cooking to ensure even crispness.
4 Place the crisp slices on a cooling tray until cold, then store in an airtight container.

play time

Make an inexpensive agility course in your back yard using garden canes, plastic hoops and chairs.

- **The weave:** Stick five garden canes in the ground in a line with gaps between them.
- **The tunnel:** For a small dog, place two or three upside-down chairs in a row; for larger breeds, use a garden bench (with no cross-bars underneath). Throw a blanket over the top to make the tunnel more exciting.
- **Hoop jump:** Hold a hoop up for your pet to jump through or attach it to a couple of garden canes with tape or string.
- **Jumps:** Use three canes to make an H-shaped jump. Secure the canes with tape or string.

origins of dog sayings

'In the doghouse'

Meaning: Out of favour; to receive punishment.
This is thought to have originated from the children's classic *Peter Pan* by J. M. Barrie (1860–1937). Mr Darling is horrible to the family's dog Nana and the children run away, so Mr Darling is made to live in the doghouse until they return home.

scrummy sweetmeat chews

Your dog is guaranteed to roll
over and beg for more of these
tasty morsels.

**250 g/8 oz piece of beefsteak
liquid honey**

1 Pre-heat the oven to 220°C/425°F/Gas
   Mark 7. Grease a baking tray or use a
   nonstick one.
2 Slice the steak into approximately
   12 cm/5 inch long, 1 cm/½ inch thick,
   1 cm/½ inch wide strips. Place them on
   the baking tray.
3 Brush the meat strips with honey and
   cook in the oven for 10 minutes. Allow to
   cool and harden.
4 Store in the refrigerator for up to three
   days and serve as an extra-special treat.

22

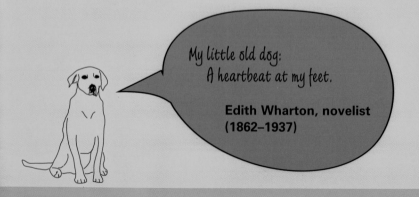

My little old dog:
   A heartbeat at my feet.

**Edith Wharton, novelist
(1862–1937)**

nutty mutt nibbles

Crumbly comestibles that melt in
the mouth – what more could a
dog ask for?

**handful of shelled pecan nuts, coarsely
chopped**
handful of shelled walnuts, coarsely chopped
handful of redskin peanuts
2 tablespoons plain wholemeal flour
125 g/4 oz/½ cup crunchy peanut butter

1 Pre-heat the oven to 150°C/300°F/Gas
   Mark 2. Grease a baking tray or use a
   nonstick one.
2 Mix all the ingredients together.
3 Form 2.5 cm/1 inch balls by gently
   rolling pieces of the mixture
   between your palms.
4 Place the balls on the
   baking tray and bake for
   25 minutes. Allow to
   cool on the baking
   tray before handling
   or serving them.

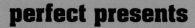

perfect presents

Dogs love getting and unwrapping presents, so put a smile on your pet's face with his very own Santa sock.

You will need:
46 cm/18 inch square of red felt
tacking pins
thick black felt-tip pen
scissors
sewing machine or needle and thread
red, gold and green ribbons

1 Fold the felt in half, with the right sides together, and pin the edges to hold them in place.

24

2 With a black pen, draw the bottom and two long sides of a big bone on one side of the felt. Use pins to outline the remaining top end of the bone.

3 Cut around the guidelines and pins so that you have two bone-shaped pieces of felt.

4 Sew around the drawn guidelines, about 5 mm/¼ inch from the edge, using small running stitches. Remove the pins from the unsewn end of the bone and turn the fabric right side out.

5 Stitch a loop of ribbon to the open end of the bone so that you can hang it up. Make the remaining ribbons into bows and stitch them on to the bone through their centres.

6 On Christmas Eve, stuff the sock with goodies and wait to be woken at the crack of dawn by your pet, eager to see what Santa has brought him.

quick trick treats

These simple snacks are perfect
training treats for in-a-hurry
hounds and their humans.

1 packet of digestive biscuits
unsalted, low-fat cottage or soft cheese
1 sweet, crunchy, red-skinned dessert apple,
  thinly sliced

1 Spread the biscuits with cheese.
2 Place an apple disc on top of
   each biscuit.

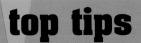

top tips

If you have a convalescing dog or puppy,
scrambled eggs is a light, nutritious and
easy-to-digest meal. Another great meal for
convalescing dogs is cooked rice and
chicken. This is easy to eat and chicken is
also lower in calories than red meat.

top dog toasties

These nut-flavoured toasties make
satisfying fillers for snack
attacks between meals.

2 slices of wholemeal or brown bread
½ tablespoon low-fat sunflower or vegetable
 spread
1 tablespoon fat-free soft cheese
4 tablespoons flaked tuna or canned dog meat
1 tablespoon crunchy peanut butter

1 Pre-heat the grill until it is red hot.
2 Toast one side of the bread until light golden brown.
 Remove from under the grill and turn the grill down to low.
3 Thinly spread the untoasted side of one slice of bread with
 sunflower or vegetable spread, then lavishly spread with soft
 cheese and tuna or dog meat. Thinly spread the untoasted
 side of the remaining slice of bread with peanut butter.
4 Sandwich the two slices of toast together and place back
 under the grill for a couple of minutes on each side until the
 toast is crisp and the filling has melted.
5 Cut diagonally into quarters, allow to cool and serve.

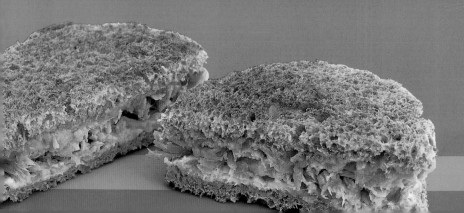

Greyfriar's Bobby

The story of Greyfriar's Bobby is a shining example of the devotion of dogs. Bobby was a young Skye Terrier who lived in Edinburgh, Scotland, in the 19th century. He became famous because he refused to be parted from his master, John Grey, even by death. For 14 years he kept vigil in Greyfriar's churchyard, sleeping on the grave of his master every night despite countless attempts to drive him away. Bobby was eventually adopted by local residents; they gave him food and he played with their children. When he died in 1872, the loyal dog was laid to rest beside his master's grave and a memorial was commissioned in his honour.

Brothers and sisters, I bid you beware.
Of giving your heart to a dog to tear.

**Rudyard Kipling, writer
(1865–1936)**

Rolling on his back

This is your dog's way of being submissive and telling you that you're the boss. He will often do this when out on walks if he meets a more dominant dog. However, he may also roll over on to his back if he is feeling happy and wants you to tickle his tummy.

28

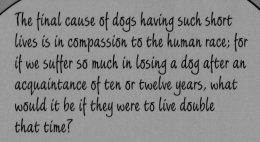

The final cause of dogs having such short lives is in compassion to the human race; for if we suffer so much in losing a dog after an acquaintance of ten or twelve years, what would it be if they were to live double that time?

Sir Walter Scott, novelist and poet (1771–1832)

fishy feasts

Your dog will go crazy for these golden-brown fish biscuit balls. Serve them whenever your pooch has been well behaved.

1 fish or meat stock cube
150 ml/¼ pint/⅔ cup boiling water
125 g/4 oz tinned flaked tuna in oil,
   drained
125 g/4 oz/1¾ cups porridge oats
50 g/2 oz/¼ cup cornmeal
6 g/¼ oz fast-action dried yeast
50 g/2 oz/½ cup plain flour
extra flour, for kneading
1 small egg, beaten

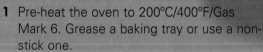

1 Pre-heat the oven to 200°C/400°F/Gas Mark 6. Grease a baking tray or use a non-stick one.
2 Dissolve the stock cube in the boiling water and allow to cool. Add the tuna, oats, cornmeal, yeast and measured flour and work into a dough.
3 Put 2 handfuls of flour on to a cool work surface and knead the dough on it until all the flour has been worked in. Allow the dough to rest for 10 minutes.
4 Cut the dough into 2.5 cm/1 inch pieces and shape into balls by gently rolling them between floury palms. Place the balls on the baking tray and brush with beaten egg.
5 Bake for 20 minutes until golden brown. Allow to cool.

scamp's stir-fry

If your dog is too small for this much grub, keep the excess in the refrigerator for another nosh-up the following day.

25 ml/1 fl oz/2 tablespoons vegetable oil
125 g/4 oz boneless chicken (raw or cooked), roughly chopped
50 g/2 oz fresh or frozen spinach
1 potato, diced
4 cherry tomatoes, quartered
2 green cabbages, roughly chopped
1 carrot, chopped
1 teaspoon garlic powder
double handful of your pet's favourite complementary mixer meal
125 ml/4 fl oz/½ cup chicken or beef stock
chopped parsley, to garnish

1 Put all the ingredients (except the mixer meal, stock and parsely) into a large frying pan or wok and stir-fry on a high heat until the vegetables are tender.
2 Put the stir-fry into a food bowl with the mixer meal.
3 Add the stock and mix together. Allow to cool.
4 Garnish with a sprinkling of parsley.

How the dog got its name

When God had made the earth and
  sky, the flowers and the trees.
He then made all the animals and all
  the birds and bees.
And when His work was finished, and
  not one was quite the same
He said I'll walk this Earth of mine and
  give each one a name.
And so He travelled land and sea, and
  everywhere He went
A little creature followed Him, until its
  strength was spent.
When all were named upon the Earth,
  and in the sky and sea,
The little creature said, Dear Lord,
  there's not one left for me.
The Father smiled and softly said,
  I've left you to the end,
I've turned my own name back to front
  and called you 'Dog', my friend.

Anonymous

Spotty & Barney

President George W. Bush and first lady Laura Bush are the proud owners of two dogs – English Springer Spaniel, Spotty, and Scottish Terrier, Barney. Spotty is the daughter of Mildred Kerr Bush, the canine author of *Millie's Book*, who belonged to former president George Bush and first lady Barbara. Apparently, Spotty and Barney's favourite sport is playing tennis with the president. Spotty's favourite food is bacon-flavoured dog treats; Barney prefers milk-flavoured ones.

top tips

Some dogs will do anything for a sweet and tender baby carrot. Fruits and vegetables make good, inexpensive and non-fattening treats but you should always rinse them first in fresh, clean, cold water to remove any pesticides. Organically grown produce is the best option for hypersensitive dogs, but still wash it first, preferably in bottled water.

paw-lickin' chicken

This is haute cuisine for
discerning dogs. Serve on its
own or with Round Hound Roasties
(see page 36).

50 g/2 oz/¼ cup low-fat sunflower spread
1 tablespoon tinned chickpeas, drained
1 tablespoon soft cheese
250 g/8 oz boneless chicken breast
1 small mushroom, sliced
1 tablespoon grated hard cheese
pinch of fennel seeds
parsley sprig and natural yogurt, to garnish

1 Pre-heat the grill to a low setting and melt the sunflower spread
  in the grill pan. Remove the pan from the grill, then turn up the
  heat to medium high.
2 Mash the chickpeas and soft cheese together to make a paste.
  Slice the chicken breast almost in half, leaving it joined at each
  end and down one side. Stuff the breast with the paste and
  mushroom slices.
3 Lay the stuffed chicken breast top-side down in the bottom of the
  pan and grill, basting once, until lightly browned. Turn the chicken
  over, baste the top and grill until it is cooked through (when the
  juices run clear and the meat is white).
4 Remove the chicken from under the grill and turn the heat down
  to low. Sprinkle the top of the breast with grated cheese and
  fennel seeds. Grill the chicken until the cheese melts, then
  allow to cool.
5 Garnish with parsley and a dollop of yogurt.

'Barking up the wrong tree'

Meaning: To misdirect your argument or efforts.
This is believed to have originated from the raccoon
hunters of the 19th century, who would take a dog out
with them when they went hunting at night. When being
pursued, a raccoon would often go up a tree in an effort to
escape. The dog's job was to sit at the bottom of the tree
and bark until his master arrived. If the dog picked the
wrong tree, the hunter was less likely to get his raccoon.

34

Pricked ears

This suggests that, for some
reason, your dog is alert and ready.
If it happens in a training class while
your dog is looking attentively at you,
then thank your lucky stars because it
means that he is paying attention and
waiting for your next command.

spaghetti doganaise

This tasty teatime treat will
get your dog's salivary glands
working overtime – and your own.

250 g/8 oz coarsely minced lean beef
125 g/4 oz mushrooms, chopped
1 small onion, chopped
5 tablespoons virgin olive oil
2 teaspoons garlic powder
200 g/7 oz canned plum tomatoes,
  chopped
1 tablespoon beef gravy granules or powder
75 g/3 oz dry wheat spaghetti
30 g/1 oz/¼ cup low-fat hard cheese, grated
parsley sprig, to garnish

1 Put the meat, mushrooms, onion, olive oil and garlic powder in a
pan and stir-fry on a medium heat for approximately 15 minutes
until the meat has browned and the onion is soft.
2 Add the tomatoes (with the juice) and bring to the boil. Reduce
the heat and simmer for 10 minutes.
3 Add the gravy granules or powder to the meat sauce, stir until
dissolved and the sauce has thickened, then remove the sauce
from the heat.
4 Cook the spaghetti as instructed on the packet. Drain and place in
a serving dish. Pour the meat sauce on top.
5 Sprinkle with grated cheese and garnish with parsley. Allow to
cool, then serve with a flourish.

round hound roasties

Serve these roasties by them-
selves as treats, or to accompany
Paw-Lickin' Chicken (see page 33)
for seriously wicked sustenance.

500 g/1 lb potatoes, quartered
2 tablespoons dried skimmed milk
250 g/8 oz lean minced beef, lamb, chicken or
turkey
50 g/2 oz/½ cup onion, finely chopped
vegetable oil, for frying and glazing
50 g/2 oz/½ cup hard cheese, grated

1 Pre-heat the oven to 220°C/425°F/Gas
Mark 7. Grease a baking tray or use a
nonstick one.
2 Place the potatoes in a pan of boiling
water and boil until soft. Drain off the
water, add the skimmed milk and mash.
3 Stir-fry the meat and onion in 2 tablespoons
of oil until the onions are soft and the meat
has browned. Drain off the juices.
4 Add the stir-fry and cheese to the mashed
potatoes and mix well. Use a tablespoon
to scoop out balls of mash and put them
on the baking tray.
5 Brush the balls with a little oil and roast in
the top of the oven until golden brown
and crisp on the outside. Allow to cool
before serving.

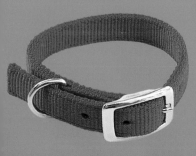

How Velcro was invented

One day in 1948, while out walking his dog, the Swiss inventor George de Mestral noticed that his pet's coat was covered in cockleburs. Out of curiosity he decided to study the burs under a microscope and, to his surprise, found that the cocklebur had a natural hook-like shape that had attached itself to a loop of the dog's hair. As a result, Velcro was invented; it was patented in 1955.

top tips

Chocolate contains a drug called theobromine, which is poisonous to dogs. Symptoms of chocolate poisoning include sickness, restlessness, rapid heartbeat and breathing, weakness, seizures and loss of consciousness. If you believe your dog has consumed chocolate, seek advice from a vet. Doggy chocs are specially made for canines and contain no theobromine, so it's safer for your four-legged chocoholic chum to stick to these.

bonzer's pitta patty burgers

Your pal will be hounding you for more of these easy-to-make beefy bites – and they'll taste good to you, too.

250 g/8 oz lean minced beef or lamb
1 small onion, finely chopped
1 egg, beaten
handful of fresh wholemeal breadcrumbs
2 tablespoons natural yogurt or unsalted
    cream cheese
2 wholemeal pitta breads

1 Pre-heat the grill to medium high.
2 Mix the meat, onion, egg and bread-crumbs together.
3 Divide the mixture in half and shape into 2 patties, about 1.5 cm/¾ inch thick. If necessary, flour your hands to stop the mixture from sticking to them.
4 Place the patties under the grill for approximately 5 minutes, then turn them over and grill for another 4 minutes, until browned and crisp on the outside and fully cooked inside. Allow to cool.
5 Top each patty with a tablespoon of yogurt or cream cheese and place into a pitta.

top tips

Put together a small first-aid kit so you can cope with any minor accidents that your pet might have in the home. In most cases it is advisable to contact your vet, so keep his or her phone number in the kit as well.

dog stars

Huckleberry Hound was the first cartoon character to be awarded an Emmy by the Television Academy.

The nose of the Bulldog has been slanted backwards so that he can breathe without letting go.

Winston Churchill, British prime minister (1874–1965)

Ears back & tail between his legs

Oh dear, someone isn't happy. This is your dog's way of showing that he's feeling scared or apprehensive about something.

dog stars

Rin Tin Tin was born in France in 1918. He was rescued by a group of American airmen and was adopted by one of his rescuers, Corporal Lee Duncan. Rin Tin Tin shot to fame in his screen debut, 'The Man from Hell's River', in 1922. He went on to make over 40 films and earned in excess of $1 million.

lentil hotpot

This protein-packed hotpot will make a fine feast for your furry friend on a cold winter's day.

125 g/4 oz/1 cup couscous
200 ml/7 fl oz/1 cup boiling water
7 teaspoons olive oil
15 g/½ oz/1 tablespoon low-fat sunflower
  spread
250 g/8 oz diced turkey
50 g/2 oz/½ cup onion, finely chopped
¼ teaspoon garlic powder
400 g/13 oz tin of green lentils, drained and
  rinsed in cold water
parsley sprig and 1 sweet cherry tomato,
  quartered, to garnish

1 Put the couscous in a pan and add the
   boiling water plus 1 teaspoon of the oil.
   Stir, then cover and stand for 5 minutes.
2 Add the sunflower spread, place the pan on
   a medium heat and cook gently for
   3 minutes. Separate the grains with a fork.
3 Stir-fry the meat, onion and garlic powder
   in the remaining oil until the onion softens.
4 Remove from the heat and mix in the
   lentils and couscous.
5 Transfer to a serving dish, allow to cool,
   then garnish with the parsely and tomato.

chunky chow

Offer this when there's a full moon to bring out the werewolf in your wondermutt.

125 g/4 oz/1 cup couscous
200 ml/7 fl oz/1 cup boiling water
1 teaspoon vegetable or olive oil
1 chicken stock cube
40 g/1½ oz/1½ tablespoons low-fat sunflower spread
250 g/8 oz turkey meat, diced
75 g/3 oz/¾ cup tinned chickpeas, drained and coarsely chopped
25 g/1 oz/¼ cup tinned red kidney beans, drained and coarsely chopped
¼ teaspoon garlic powder
1 tablespoon natural yogurt
1 tablespoon dried skimmed milk
parsley sprig, to garnish

1 Place the couscous in a pan and add the boiling water, oil and crumbled stock cube. Stir, then cover and stand for 5 minutes.
2 Add 15 g/½ oz of the sunflower spread, place on a medium heat, cook gently for 3 minutes. Separate couscous grains with a fork.
3 Melt the remaining sunflower spread in another pan and add the turkey, chickpeas, kidney beans and garlic powder. Stir-fry until the meat has browned.
4 Remove from the heat and stir in the yogurt and milk.
5 Place the couscous around the edge of a bowl, place the meat mixture in the middle and garnish with parsley. Serve when cool.

Royal dogs

Queen Elizabeth II is a devoted dog owner but is probably best known for her love of Corgis. Her first Corgi, Susan, was given to her as an 18th birthday present in 1944 and, during her reign, she has owned more than 30 Corgis. She currently has four, called Swift, Emma, Linnet and Pharos. Not content with Corgis, the Queen also introduced a new breed of dog called a Dorgi – a cross between a Corgi and a Dachshund. There have been eight Dorgis – Harris, Tinker, Brandy, Cider, Berry, Piper, Chipper and Pickles.

You think dogs will not be in heaven? I tell you, they will be there long before any of us.

Robert Louis Stevenson, writer (1850–94)

top tips

Sugar-free breakfast cereals with milk are easy-to-make and yummy meals for your pet. They are also an excellent source of vitamins.

rover's risotto

This deliciously quick-to-make supper is ideal for dogs (and owners) who have difficulty chewing. Your dog will find them moreishly mouth-watering!

50 g/2 oz/½ cup long-grain easy-cook brown rice
50 g/2 oz/½ cup red split lentils
1 chicken stock cube
175 ml/6 fl oz/¾ cup boiling water
50 g/2 oz/¼ cup sunflower spread
1 small mushroom, chopped
125 g/4 oz minced turkey
50 g/2 oz/½ cup onion, finely chopped
2–3 crisp lettuce leaves
1 sweet cherry tomato, quartered, to garnish

44

1 Put the rice, lentils and stock cube into a small pan with the boiling water.
2 Bring back to the boil and simmer until the rice and lentils are soft (approximately 7–10 minutes) and have absorbed the water. Stir frequently to prevent sticking.
3 Melt the sunflower spread in a larger pan and add the mushroom, turkey and onion. Stir-fry until the onions are soft and the meat has browned.
4 Add the rice and lentils to the pan of meat and stir. Allow to cool.
5 Serve on a bed of lettuce leaves and garnish with tomato.

perfect presents

Dogs love it when you throw things for them and they adore following scent trails. Fetch-it Fido is an aniseed-scented denim toy that is ideal for playing hide-and-seek or fetch. This gift is easy to make and will keep your dog happy for hours.

You will need:
2 x 30 cm/12 inch squares of strong material
(old denim jeans are ideal)
tacking pins
sewing machine or needle and thread
old socks or other material to stuff the toy
aniseed food flavouring

1 Put the squares of fabric on top of each other (if one side of each is rough, put these on the outside).
2 Tack three sides of the denim fabric together with pins about 1.5 cm/¾ inch from the edge. Sew along the three sides about 5 mm/¼ inch from the edge.
3 Remove the pins and turn the material right side out.
4 Stuff the material with old socks, or some other filling, and shake a few drops of aniseed food flavouring inside, then sew up the remaining open side of the square.
5 Show your dog his new toy and let him have a good sniff. Then, play! You can play throw and fetch games – it makes a great training toy – or you can hide it and let him search it out and bring it back to you for lots of well-earned praise and a pat.

growling grub pie

What could be better after a wintry walk than a tasty tummy warmer. Your dog will growl with delight.

500 g/1 lb potatoes, quartered
1 beef stock cube
300 ml/½ pint/1¼ cups boiling water
250 g/8 oz minced lean beef
50 g/2 oz/½ cup carrot, diced
50 g/2 oz/½ cup onion, chopped
¼ teaspoon dried parsley
¼ teaspoon dried thyme
1 tablespoon beef gravy granules or powder
2 tablespoons grated hard cheese
parsley sprig, to garnish

1 Pre-heat the oven to 200°C/400°F/Gas Mark 6. Grease a 1.2 litre/ 2 pint ovenproof dish.

2 Place the potatoes in a pan of boiling water. Boil until soft, then drain and mash.

3 In another pan, dissolve the stock cube in the measured boiling water, then add the beef, carrot, onion, parsley and thyme. Bring to the boil and simmer until the onions are soft. Add the gravy granules or powder to thicken, then pour into a serving dish.

4 Spoon the potatoes on top of the meat and gently fork over to roughen the surface of the potatoes. Sprinkle on the cheese. Bake in the oven for 20 minutes or until the cheese has melted. Brown under a red-hot grill to form a crust, if required.

5 Garnish with parsley and allow to cool before serving.

pooch pasta

There'll be clean dishes every time with this meaty beanfeast – it's tasty, filling and gives a dog plenty to chew on.

125 g/4 oz dry pasta twists
400 g/13 oz tinned dog meat
handful of drained tinned blackeye beans
handful of drained tinned red kidney beans
double handful of cornflakes
½ handful of redskin peanuts and 1 sweet
   cherry tomato, cut into eighths, to garnish

1 Place the pasta in boiling water and simmer until soft. Drain and allow to cool.
2 Put the pasta in a bowl, add the dog meat, beans and cornflakes and mix together.
3 Transfer to a serving dish and garnish with peanuts and tomato.

doggy trivia

The oldest dog

An Australian Cattle-dog called Bluey holds the record for being the oldest documented dog. He was 29 years and 5 months when he died - that's over 200 doggy years.

48

pooches in print

Oliver Twist

Bull's-eye is the canine companion of Bill Sikes in Charles Dickens's *Oliver Twist*, which was published in instalments from 1837 to 1839. Portrayed as a Bull Terrier in the book and as a Staffordshire Bull Terrier in film and musical versions, the dog is described by Dickens as 'A white shaggy dog, with his face scratched and torn in 20 different places...' Bull's-eye endured a great deal at the hands of his master but, despite being shouted at and kicked, he followed Sikes with total devotion. When Sikes is killed, Bull's-eye falls to his own death trying to reach his master.

top tips

Does your pet refuse to pay attention during training sessions and prefer to spend his time playing? Take him out to play before you start any training. He will get rid of all that excess energy and should be more attentive in class.

meaty muscle builder

Build your mutt's muscles with this iron-rich ragout that'll put more hairs on his chest, a spring in his whiskers and a curl in his tail.

50 g/2 oz frozen or fresh minced lamb, beef, chicken or turkey
125 g/4 oz frozen green leaf spinach
1 meat stock cube
¼ teaspoon garlic powder
250 ml/8 fl oz/1 cup cold water
25 g/1 oz/¼ cup bulgar wheat
½ handful of grated fresh carrot
   and parsley sprig, to garnish

1 Put the meat, spinach, stock cube, garlic and water in a pan and bring to the boil on a high heat.
2 Once boiling, turn the heat down to medium and simmer rapidly for 10 minutes.
3 Turn the heat to low, add the bulgar wheat and gently simmer for another 10 minutes or until all the water has been absorbed. Remove from the heat and allow to cool.
4 Transfer to a serving dish and garnish with carrot and parsley.

doganettos

It's nice to cool off your canine chum on hot summer days with fruit-flavoured frozen yogurt. Serve it in a bowl or a wafer cone.

½ ripe banana or other favourite fruit, mashed
4 drops of vanilla food flavouring
250 g/8 oz/1 cup low-fat natural yogurt
wafer cone, to serve (optional)

1 Mix the fruit, vanilla flavouring and yogurt together.
2 Pour the mixture into a freezer-safe plastic tub, put on the lid and freeze.
3 Cut the frozen mixture into treat-sized chunks or serve in a wafer cone.

dog stars

Adored by his owner Bart Simpson, Santa's Little Helper enjoys a lifestyle most dogs only dream of. Not only does he get to eat from the table, but he also manages to get away with tearing up the furniture.

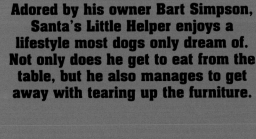

doggy trivia

Skydiving sausage dog

The highest skydiving dog in the world is a Miniature Dachshund called Brutus, who skydived (accompanied by his owner, of course) over California from an incredible 4,500 metres/15,000 feet in May 1997. He has performed a total of 71 skydives so far. Brutus beat the previous record of British Jack Russell Katie, the first dog to be caught by the skydiving bug when she jumped in 1987. The first canine parachute jump (in fact the first parachute jump by a living creature) took place in the 18th century when Frenchman J. P. Blanchard dropped a dog from a hot-air balloon in a basket to which a parachute was attached.

Confrontational approach

Careful does it! If your dog faces another dog or a person with his hackles raised, direct eye contact and raised tail and ears, it can mean one of two things: either your dog is demonstrating his dominance or he's about to attack.

'Raining cats and dogs'

Meaning: To rain heavily.
The author Jonathan Swift used the phrase in his book *Polite and Ingenious Conversation* (1738), which suggests that it was actually a much older saying. One thought is that thunder and lightning are like a cat-and-dog fight. Another explanation is that the dog was a symbol of the wind in mythology, while the cat was thought to have an influence on the weather.

crunchy cornflake cakes

Go on, spoil your hairy hound with these lip-smackingly sweet treats - you can be sure he'll keep coming back for more.

40 g/1½ oz/3 tablespoons sunflower or
   vegetable oil spread
50 g/2 oz/¼ cup demerara sugar
1 small egg, beaten
50 g/2 oz/½ cup plain flour
double handful of cornflakes, lightly crushed

1 Pre-heat the oven to 190°C/375°F/Gas Mark 5. Grease a baking tray or use a nonstick one.
2 Cream the sunflower or vegetable oil spread and sugar together until light and fluffy.
3 Add the egg and sieve in the flour. Stir together lightly but well.
4 Roll teaspoonfuls of the mixture in the crushed cornflakes.
5 Place the balls on the baking tray and cook for 10–15 minutes. Transfer to a rack and allow to cool.

pooches in print

My little dog

I'll never hurt my little dog
But stroke and pat his head;
I like to see him wag his tail
I like to see him fed.

Poor little thing, how very good
And very useful too;
For do you know that he will mind
What he is bid to do?

I will never hurt my dog
And never give him pain
But treat him kindly every day
And he'll love me again.

Anonymous

doggy trivia

Diddy dogs

The smallest dog ever recorded is a Yorkshire Terrier with the strange name of Big Boss. The little dog is owned by Dr Chai Khanchanakom of Bangkok, Thailand. On Big Boss's first birthday in December 1995, the petit pooch measured a tiny 11.94 cm/4.7 inches tall and 12.95 cm/5.1 inches) long, which is only slightly larger than a fully grown hamster.

'woof it down' walnut cake

Bake this for your four-legged
friend and wait to be thanked with
hairy hugs and slobbery kisses.

2 small eggs
4 overflowing tablespoons liquid honey
5 tablespoons vegetable oil
275 g/9 oz/2¼ cups plain wholemeal flour
140 g/5 oz/1 cup carrot, grated
handful of shelled walnut pieces
handful of sultanas
handful of desiccated coconut
small pot of natural yogurt or
   unsalted soft cheese
doggy chocs, to decorate

1 Pre-heat the oven to 180°C/350°F/Gas Mark 4.
   Grease a cake tin.
2 Mix the eggs, honey and oil together in a
   large bowl until smooth. Sieve in the flour,
   then add the carrot, walnuts, sultanas and
   coconut. Fold together to make a smooth
   mixture, then pour into the cake tin.
3 Bake for approximately 40 minutes. Insert a
   metal skewer in the middle of the cake and
   pull it out. If it comes out clean, the cake is
   cooked. Allow to cool on a rack.
4 Frost with yogurt or soft cheese and
   decorate with doggy chocs. Store in an airtight container.

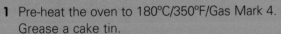

furry pupcakes

These dainty delicacies are perfect for fussy pups. You could also bake a larger version for a puppy birthday party.

2 small eggs, beaten
6 drops vanilla food flavouring
½ ripe banana, mashed
6 tablespoons cold water
125 g/4 oz/1 cup white self-raising flour
25 g/1 oz/¼ cup plain wholemeal flour
1 tablespoon demerara sugar
handful of sunflower seeds
¼ teaspoon cinnamon
1 tablespoon dried skimmed milk
mascarpone cheese and doggy chocs,
    to decorate

1 Pre-heat the oven to 180°C/350°F/Gas Mark 4.
2 Cream the eggs, vanilla flavouring, banana and water together in a mixing bowl. Lightly fold in all the dry ingredients.
3 Spoon the mixture into paper cupcake cases so that they are half full and place on a baking tray.
4 Bake for 35 minutes or until light brown (test if they are ready by inserting a metal skewer through the middle of the cakes; if it comes out clean, the pupcakes are ready). Allow to cool on a rack.
5 Decorate each cake with 1 teaspoon of mascarpone cheese and a doggy choc.

prized possessions

Solomon & Sophie

Talk-show host and personality Oprah Winfrey is the proud owner of a chocolate American Cocker Spaniel called Solomon and a black American Cocker Spaniel called Sophie. Oprah's pets are an important part of her life and have regularly been on her chat show during pet-orientated features. In fact, when she was once asked about her dogs, she is reported to have said: 'What dogs?! These are my children, little people with fur who make my heart open a little wider.'

top tips

If your dog keeps chewing things he shouldn't, he could be bored. Stimulate his mind (and his stomach) with an interactive toy such as a Kong. This is a rubber toy with a hole through the middle that you can fill with some of the healthy treats from this book. Not only will it keep him amused, but it could also stop him from wrecking your house.

historical dogs

Fido

President Abraham Lincoln's dog was called Fido. He was described as 'a floppy-eared, rough-coated yellowish dog of uncertain origin'. When Lincoln was elected president, he decided not to take the dog to Washington because he was concerned that Fido would not survive the long train journey from Illinois.

58

dog stars

Lassie was created by Eric Knight in his book 'Lassie Come Home' and first appeared on the silver screen in the 1943 MGM film of the book. The courageous Rough Collie was in fact a male dog called Pal, owned and trained by Rudd Weatherwax. Pal took over from the chosen Collie bitch when she failed to perform.

barker's birthday cake

Celebrate your pal's extra-
special day in style by baking
this cool canine confection.

175 g/6 oz/1½ cups self-raising wholemeal flour
50 g/2 oz/¼ cup demerara sugar
2 tablespoons dried skimmed milk
2 small eggs, beaten
5 tablespoons cold water
handful of sultanas
2 overflowing tablespoons liquid honey
4 overflowing tablespoons/½ cup mascarpone
cheese
doggy chocs, birthday candles and holders,
to decorate

1 Pre-heat the oven to 180°C/350°F/Gas Mark 4. Grease two
18 cm/7 inch round cake tins.
2 Put all the ingredients (except the honey, cheese and doggy chocs)
in a bowl and fold together to make a light, airy mixture. Divide the
mixture into the cake tins and bake in the middle of the oven for
30 minutes. Pierce the middle of each cake with a metal skewer; if
it comes out clean, they are cooked. Allow to cool on a wire rack.
3 Use a sharp knife to level off the top of one cake.
4 Mix the honey and 3 tablespoons of the cheese together and
spread the mixture on the levelled cake. Place the other cake on
top and frost it with the remaining cheese.
5 Decorate the cake with doggy chocs and the appropriate number
of candles. Don't forget to tell your dog to make a wish as you
blow out the candles.

bow-wow cake

Your favourite Fido can't fail to
be charmed by this deliciously
fruity cheesecake.

10 digestive biscuits
45 g/1½ oz/3 tablespoons sunflower spread
150 g/5 oz/⅔ cup fat-free soft cheese
thin slices of ripe mango, banana, grape,
**   apple or other fresh fruit, to decorate**
1 tablespoon demerara sugar

1 Lightly grease or line a 15 cm/6 inch
   serving dish.
2 Put the biscuits into a plastic food bag
   and crush them with a rolling pin.
3 Melt the sunflower spread in a saucepan
   over a low heat. Pour it into a mixing
   bowl, add the crushed biscuits and
   combine well.
4 Spread the mixture into the bottom of
   the dish, then cover the biscuit base with
   the cheese.
5 Decorate the top of the cheesecake with
   slices of fruit, then sprinkle with sugar.
   Chill in a refrigerator until set.

Peter Pan

Nana, the Newfoundland in J. M. Barrie's classic children's book *Peter Pan* (1911), was based on the author's own Newfoundland called Luath. Readers meet Nana at the beginning of the book when Mr and Mrs Darling employ her as their children's nurse because they cannot afford a human one. Nana proves to be a very good nurse. It is only when Mr Darling makes her sleep outside, instead of in her kennel in the nursery, that Peter Pan manages to fly the Darling children off to Neverland.

Histories are more full of examples of the fidelity of dogs than of friends.

**Alexander Pope, poet
(1688–1744)**

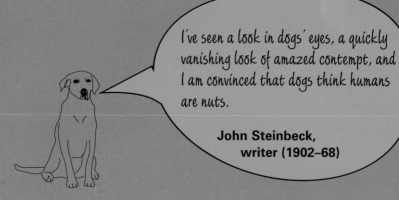

I've seen a look in dogs' eyes, a quickly vanishing look of amazed contempt, and I am convinced that dogs think humans are nuts.

**John Steinbeck,
writer (1902–68)**

top tips

Avoid giving your dog poultry bones because they are prone to splintering. Being small, poultry bones can also get stuck in the throat and cause choking, or become wedged in the roof of the mouth and cause discomfort...

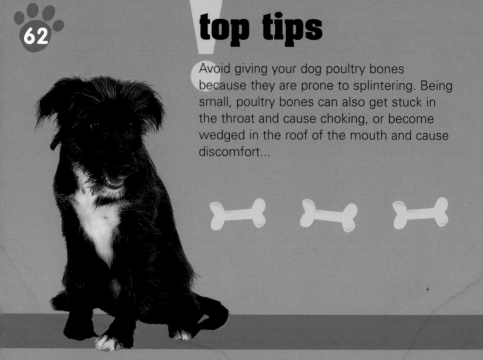

mutt's milky pudding

This milky rice pudding is a
dessert to drool for — among
dogs and owners alike.

600 ml/1 pint/2½ cups skimmed milk
40 g/1½ oz/⅓ cup short-grain (pudding)
  rice
25 g/1 oz/1 tablespoon low-fat sunflower
  spread
40 g/1½ oz/3 tablespoons demerara sugar
pinch of grated nutmeg

1 Pre-heat the oven to 150°C/300°F/Gas
  Mark 2. Grease a 1.2 litre/2 pint ovenproof dish.
2 Place the milk, rice, sunflower spread
  and sugar in a dish. Sprinkle the
  nutmeg on top.
3 Bake in the oven for 2½–3 hours,
  stirring twice during the first hour.
4 Allow to cool before serving.

index of recipes

acknowledgements

Octopus Publishing Group Limited/Stephen Conroy 8, 11, 13 top left, 14, 17, 20, 23, 26, 29, 30, 35, 36, 38, 42, 46, 49, 50, 53, 56, 59, 60, 63/Steve Gorton 7, 10, 13 centre right, 34, 40, 52, 57, 58/Rosie Hyde 2, 15, 25, 32, 37, 45, 64/Tim Ridley 19, 55, 62. jacket pictures: **Getty Images/Stone** back cover bottom. **Octopus Publishing Group Limited**/Rosie Hyde front cover top right, front cover centre left, back cover top right, /Stephen Conroy back cover centre left.

Commissioning Editor: Sarah Ford
Senior Editor: Clare Churly
Copy-editor: Michelle Pickering
Senior Designer: Joanna Bennett
Designer: Geoff Borin
Production Controller: Lucy Woodhead
Special photography: Stephen Conroy
Food Stylist: David Morgan